P9-CEJ-709

Uncharted, Unexplored, and Unexplained

Scientific Advancements of the 19th Century

Henry Bessemer
Making Steel from Iron

Mitchell Lane
PUBLISHERS

P.O. Box 196
Hockessin, Delaware
19707

Uncharted, Unexplored, and Unexplained

Scientific Advancements of the 19th Century

Titles in the Series

Visit us on the web: www.mitchelllane.com
Comments? email us: mitchelllane@mitchelllane.com

Uncharted, Unexplored, and Unexplained

Scientific Advancements of the 19th Century

Henry Bessemer

Making Steel from Iron

Kathleen Tracy

Uncharted, Unexplored, and Unexplained

Scientific Advancements of the 19th Century

Mitchell Lane
PUBLISHERS

Copyright © 2006 by Mitchell Lane Publishers, Inc. All rights reserved. No part of this book may be reproduced without written permission from the publisher. Printed and bound in the United States of America.

Printing   1   2   3   4   5   6   7   8   9

Library of Congress Cataloging-in-Publication Data
Tracy, Kathleen.
    Henry Bessemer: making steel from iron / by Kathleen Tracy.
        p. cm. —(Uncharted, unexplored, and unexplained: scientific advancements of the 19th century)
    Includes bibliographical references and index.
    ISBN 1-58415-366-0 (lib. bdg.)
    1. Bessemer, Henry, Sir, 1813-1898—Juvenile literature. 2. Metallurgists—England—Biography. 3. Inventors—England—Juvenile literature. 4. Bessemer process—Juvenile literature. I. Title II. Uncharted, unexplored, and unexplained.
    TN140.B5T73 2005
    669'.092—dc22
                                                            2005004253

ABOUT THE AUTHOR: Kathleen Tracy has been a journalist for over 20 years. Her writing has been featured in magazines such as *The Toronto Star*'s "Star Week," *A&E Biography* magazine, *KidScreen* and *TV Times*. She is also the author of numerous biographies, including *The Boy Who Would Be King* (Dutton), *Jerry Seinfeld—The Entire Domain* (Carol Publishing), *Don Imus—America's Cowboy* (Carroll and Graf), and *Mariano Guadalupe Vallejo, William Hewlett: Pioneer of the Computer Age*, and *Top Secret: The Story of the Manhattan Project* (Mitchell Lane Publishers). She recently completed *Diana Rigg: The Biography* (Benbella Books).

Uncharted, Unexplored, and Unexplained

Scientific Advancements of the 19th Century

Henry Bessemer

Making Steel from Iron

The 10,100-ton Eiffel Tower, completed in 1889, was made of iron. Although iron was strong and allowed for tall buildings, it had many drawbacks. It rusted easily and was so heavy it was often difficult to work with. Henry Bessemer's discovery of how to mass-produce lightweight, non-rusting steel would lead to modern skyscrapers.

1

Reaching for the Sky

The desire to build tall structures is almost as old as civilization. Approximately four thousand years ago, Egyptians built towering pyramids for their rulers. The ancient Greeks and Aztecs built magnificent temples to their gods. In Europe during the Middle Ages and the Renaissance, many towers were erected, such as the famed Leaning Tower of Pisa, built in 1173. All these were made of stone. One of the first structures to change the way people viewed architecture was the Eiffel Tower, which was made of iron. At the time it was built, 1887 to 1889, the Eiffel Tower was the largest freestanding structure in the world.

Building the Eiffel Tower was just one step in an architectural and industrial revolution. The end of the 19th century was a time of amazing human advances. Between 1880 and 1900, populations in American cities increased by 15 million people. Many of the newcomers immigrated from other countries all around the world, such as China, Ireland, and Italy. Others migrated from rural areas in America. All came in search of the increased job opportunities offered by America's industrial expansion.

As a result of their booming growth, U.S. cities underwent a striking, sudden transformation. Almost overnight, it was necessary to build and establish better infrastructure systems capable of handling the basic needs of so many people, including mass transit, sanitation, and—most importantly—housing and commercial business space. As cities such as New York began to run out of space on the ground and real estate prices soared, the obvious solution was to expand up. Architects began creating more economically efficient space by constructing taller buildings.

Initially the height of buildings was limited by both practicality and technology. Prior to the mid-19th century, structures over six stories high were rare because it was impractical to have people walk up so many flights of stairs. In addition, water pressure of the day was limited, so people living over 50 feet up could not get running water. Finally, the sheer weight of larger buildings posed engineering problems, because the materials used could support only so much of a load.

The first breakthrough was the invention of the hydraulic elevator by Elisha Graves Otis in 1852; and more powerful water pumps engineered at about the same time solved the problem of running water. When Englishman Henry Bessemer developed a process for cheaply mass-producing steel, buildings were finally able to reach into the sky.

In general, buildings of up to about four stories high are supported entirely by their walls. Taller buildings need some sort of supporting frame; on this frame, the walls can hang. Using steel, new construction techniques were developed that allowed engineers to design previously unimaginably tall structures.

In 1884, architect William Le Baron Jenney designed the first skyscraper to use a steel skeleton frame. Jenney discovered that thin pieces of steel could support weight just as well as thick stone walls could. With this advancement, the facade, or the material used to make the outer portion of the building, no longer had to carry the weight of the building. Now buildings could be faced with glass, chrome, or other lighter-weight materials. It also allowed for more room on each floor. Jenney's 10-story structure, Chicago's Home Insurance Company Building, was completed a year later and ushered in a new age of "skyscrapers," a term coined to denote any building at least 10 stories tall. As a result of his innovations, Jenney is credited with being the father of the modern skyscraper.

George A. Fuller introduced the next architectural innovation. In 1889, he built the Tacoma Building. Instead of using Jenney's steel skeleton frame, Fuller created "cages" using steel beams. These interconnected cages carried the building's weight. By the 1890s, skyscrapers were starting to change the skyline of nearly every major American city.

The architectural revolution of the late 19th century was only one example of how steel radically changed our daily lives. Since Bessemer developed his process, steel has become the single most important and adaptable material used in industry. Not only is it relatively cheap, it is durable and dependable. Without steel, many of the technological advances since that time would not have been possible. These include railroads, cars, the space program, the great pipelines, and even the lightweight cookware used in our kitchens.

Steel is also environmentally friendlier than many other industrial products. For example, extracting iron from ore to produce steel requires 25 percent less energy than extracting aluminum. Steel, like aluminum, is also recyclable, an ever more important issue as mankind runs out of space to dump refuse.

Since Bessemer's time, technology has allowed steel manufacturers to create stronger and more versatile grades, or types, of steel. All together, around 2,000 grades of steel have been developed for increasingly specialized uses.

Despite the unquestioned importance of steel in our daily lives, it is doubtful Henry Bessemer could have imagined just how he would change the world when he set out to find a simple, inexpensive method to produce this sought-after building material.

The Hittite Empire was located in Anatolia, which is modern-day Turkey between the Mediterranean and Black Seas. Nobody knows exactly where the Hittites originally lived, only that they arrived in the area sometime around 1900 B.C.

As the Hittite civilization advanced, they conquered the Babylonians and extended their empire into Mesopotamia, the area located between the Tigris and Euphrates Rivers that is now known as Iraq. The Hittites also began to challenge Egypt for land and trade routes. They waged a long war that eventually ended with the adoption of the first known peace treaty.

One reason the Hittites were able to challenge the larger kingdom of Egypt so successfully was because they had discovered a secret. The area settled by the Hittites was rich in iron ore. Iron, a chemical element, is a hard metal found in many mineral compounds. Early in their civilization, the Hittites discovered how to extract iron

Hittite migration around 1200 B.C.

from ore, which enabled them to make better tools and weapons than those cultures still using bronze. Although iron was more difficult to work with, it was also harder than bronze, and the edges could be made sharper. The oldest known weapon made of iron is a dagger found in Egypt that is believed to be of Hittite origin and was made about 1350 B.C.

For nearly four hundred years, the Hittites kept their iron-making techniques a secret from their neighbors and enemies and carefully restricted the export of iron weapons. But after the mysterious downfall of the Hittite Empire around 1200 B.C., ironsmiths migrated across Europe and into Asia and Africa, taking their knowledge with them. Other cultures such as the Greek, Assyrian, and Egyptian quickly embraced this new technology. As a result, the Bronze Age gave way to Iron Age. Since about 1000 B.C., iron has been the most used metal on earth.

Henry Bessemer as a successful inventor and businessman, around 1870

2

Inquisitive by Nature

Being an inventor was literally in Henry Bessemer's blood. It started when his father, Anthony, who had been born in England, was a young boy. At the age of 11, Anthony moved to Holland with his family. When old enough, he trained to be a mechanical engineer and worked on building the Netherlands' first steam engine.

Anthony Bessemer moved to Paris when he was 21. There he became a member of the Academy of Sciences in recognition of improvements he made to microscope design. While working at the Paris mint, where coins and other metal objects were made, he invented a machine called a portrait lathe, which shaped the metal.

When the French Revolution broke out in 1789, there were food shortages throughout the country. Because he and his wife lived on a small estate 20 miles outside of Paris, Anthony had sacks of wheat secretly delivered to his house for making bread. He was afraid that if people knew he had supplies, they would mob his house.

With the situation in France growing worse, Anthony Bessemer was desperate to go back to the safety of England. But because of the ongoing revolution, it was difficult to get his money out of the banks. Even when he did, the money had very little value because France was so far in debt. Finally, the Bessemers were able to escape to England. When they arrived, they had practically no money and none of their possessions, which they had had to leave in France.

Anthony Bessemer was forced to start over again. He had experience working with dies, which are metal blocks that have the shape of the desired design indented into the flat side. He started a business making gold chains of his own designs. He took the chains to local jewelers, and before long the chains were selling as fast as he could make them.

From there Anthony used the skills he had learned at the Paris mint to go to work at the Caslon Type Foundry in London. There he designed original typefaces for the owner, Henry Caslon. A collection of typefaces of the alphabet and numerals are called a font, such as what is found on a computer's word processing program.

Soon he had enough money to buy a small estate in the village of Charlton in Hertfordshire County, which is about 30 miles from the center of London. It was there, on January 19, 1813, that Henry Bessemer was born. Because Anthony had grown so close to his employer, they named their son after Henry Caslon, who also became the baby's godfather.

Eventually, Anthony started his own business with Caslon's former partner. The foundry was built right on the Charlton estate. From a young age, Henry was fascinated by his father's work and tried to learn as much of the business as he could. Henry would later write in his autobiography that it was this experience of working with metals in the foundry that fueled his interest in metallurgy—the study of metals and developing uses for them. This interest would last his entire life.

In order to make metal typefaces like Anthony Bessemer made for his employer, the metal is melted. The molten metal is then poured into a mold, which is cooled. The building where metal is melted and cast is called a foundry.

More interested in metalwork than schoolwork, Henry begged his father to let him quit school and start apprenticing to "learn something of practical engineering." His father agreed and, according to Bessemer's autobiography, "as a preliminary step he bought me one of those beautiful small slide-rest lathes. . . . After a year or two at the vice [sic] and lathe, and other practical mechanical work, my father allowed me to employ myself in making working models. . . . Among these, I well remember, was a machine for making bricks, which was one of the most successful of my early attempts, producing pretty little model bricks in white pipeclay."[1]

The foundry gave Henry a supply of molten, or melted, metal. The teenager used this to make "casting wheels, pulleys, and other parts of mechanical models where strength was not much required. . . . By some intuitive instinct modeling came to me unsought and unstudied. Often during my evening walks round the fields, with a favorite dog, I would take a small lump of yellow clay from the roadside, and fashion it into some grotesque head or natural object, from which I would afterwards make a mould and cast it in type-metal."[2]

Because there was so much competition among type foundries, Anthony Bessemer kept his unique metal compounds a strict secret, even from his son. But the inquisitive Henry was determined to know everything about his father's business. Every two months the metal from which Anthony made his typefaces was created. Henry would sneak into the foundry to see how it was done. He discovered that his father's secret for making his typefaces so much more durable was to add little amounts of tin and copper.

Henry paid for this knowledge. On more than one occasion he got violently ill from breathing in the dust produced during the process.

Henry was also interested in all types of machinery. When he wasn't at his father's foundry, he would spend hours at the flour mill, watching how the mill was powered by running water. Although he didn't know exactly what he would do for a career, he was sure it would have to do with machinery and metals.

At 17, Henry, now a mild-mannered young man over six feet tall, was about to start a new chapter in his life. Anthony had decided to move his foundry business into the city, taking his family with him. Because transportation was difficult in those days, Henry had never been out of his home village. There he enjoyed the freedom of taking walks and not encountering another living soul. He was completely unprepared for life in a bustling metropolis such as London.

Henry arrived in London on May 4, 1830. He wrote in his autobiography that it was like stepping into a different world. "I was overwhelmed with wonder and astonishment; all the ideal scenes in the *Arabian Nights*, which had held me spellbound in my native village, were as nothing to the ceaseless panorama which London presented, with its thousands of vehicles and pedestrians, its gorgeous shops and stately buildings, and its endless miles of streets and numerous squares. I was never tired of walking about, for every turn presented some new object to rivet my attention."[3]

Bessemer spent his entire first week in London walking from morning until night, exploring every street and area he could find until he was so exhausted he had to go home. Despite all the people filling the streets and parks, Henry felt miserably alone: he knew nobody and was a stranger in everyone's eyes. Unlike the people in his home village, Londoners didn't take the time to extend a greeting as they passed in the street.

Wondering how he would ever fulfill all the dreams he had, Bessemer wrote dejectedly, "Here amidst the countless thousands I stood alone, as much uncared for as the lamp-post beside me. How often I thought, in those early days in London, Shall I ever be known here? Shall I ever have the pleasure of seeing a smile of recognition light up the face of any person in these ceaseless streams of unsympathetic strangers?"[4]

Little did Henry know that not only would he be known in London, but one day his name would be known all over the world.

At the beginning of the 19th century, when Henry Bessemer was growing up, children were not required to go to school. That's why Henry was easily able to stop going and start working with his father. Educators such as Horace Mann in Massachusetts and Henry Barnard in Connecticut pushed for what they called common school reform. Their efforts eventually led to the public school system currently in the United States.

In 1852, Massachusetts became the first state to pass a law making education compulsory, or required, for children. It would be 70 more years before it became a national policy. Children from wealthy families were either sent to private school or were taught at home by tutors. Poor kids were often taught by their parents, or they might be sent to a neighbor. Many kids who lived on farms were never taught at all because their parents needed them to help out working in the fields.

Henry Barnard

As the population in an area grew, the local citizens would build a log schoolhouse. The school was usually just a one-room building, and kids would have to work by the sunlight coming in from the few windows the schoolhouse had. Their "desks" were shelves attached to the walls, and they would sit on wooden benches or stools. Because there was no electricity, the schoolhouses tended to be hot when the weather was warm. Even though most had fireplaces, they were still cold and damp in the winter.

Since there was only one room, children of various ages would be taught together. The younger ones sat in front, close to the teacher, with the older children in back. Most teachers were men. Women could also teach—but only if they were single. They were no longer allowed to teach once they were married. Many of the male teachers were former soldiers who needed work after leaving the army. All the parents who had kids in school chipped in to pay the teacher's salary. If they couldn't afford cash, they paid in food or other goods.

In rural schools, because few teachers had any proper training, children just learned "the three Rs"—reading, (w)riting, and (a)rithmetic. Books were scarce, so quite often children were taught to read using only the Bible. Kids attending larger schools were also taught other subjects such as history, grammar, geography, science, and in some cases foreign languages. To write, kids used quills, which were sharpened goose feathers, dipped in ink.

Teachers were very strict and bad behavior was not tolerated. Children could be paddled or, if they were tardy, be forced to wait outside even in the freezing cold. One of the most feared punishments was called the peg. The teacher would pinch the student's hair in a clip that was pegged, or attached, to the wall. The peg was high enough that the child would have to stand on tiptoes or his or her hair would be painfully pulled. The peg was very effective; few kids ever misbehaved again after enduring that punishment.

London's Trafalgar Square was built to commemorate the 1805 Battle of Trafalgar. The victory was the last battle for Admiral Horatio Nelson, Britain's greatest naval hero. Designer John Nash cleared the area to build the square around 1820, ten years before Bessemer arrived in London. Construction was ongoing. The National Gallery art museum (background, left), was built in 1837; Nelson's Column (foreground) was completed in 1843. The scene above was photographed around 1890.

3

A Prolific Inventor

Because he had chosen to drop out of school, Henry Bessemer found himself living in London without a trade or formal education. However, the knowledge that he had gained from working with his father would prove invaluable. Realizing that wasting time feeling sorry for himself would only make his situation worse, Henry became determined to find a way to use the skills he already possessed.

During his wanderings through the streets of London, he had met a man who was trying to sell plaster casts of medallions, which are a type of commemorative medal that can look like a large coin. Henry had bought some of the casts, thinking he could mold some medallions out of metal. Later, however, it occurred to him that he could create his own designs using things like animals or vegetables. The process required several steps.

First, Bessemer would dip into a plaster of paris mixture whatever object (or a clay model of the object) he wanted to cast. After the mold was dry, he heated it at a high temperature to incinerate whatever was inside the mold. Then he would cut a small opening in the mold and shake out the ash. He used that same opening to pour in the liquefied metal. Once it cooled, Bessemer would then break away the plaster of paris mold and be left with the metal cast.

However, when he tried to make a cast out of a more delicate object—specifically, a rose—the flower's fragile leaves broke off when he tried to remove the mold. Bessemer finally came up with an ingenious solution. He added brick dust, which made the plaster of paris more brittle once it dried, and the mold was easier to remove.

Once he had figured that out, Bessemer set out to improve his castings by using metals that would produce colors other than white. Brass didn't work, but he was able to coat a delicate layer of copper over the original castings. When working with medallions, Bessemer sometimes used a greenish blue pigment called verdigris to give it the appearance of having been made with antique bronze. When he had created enough items to properly showcase his abilities, Bessemer arranged to have an exhibit of his work at a museum in London's in Trafalgar Square.

Several businesses expressed interest in Bessemer's work but nothing led to any commissions. Then a well-known sculptor bought a bust he had made of William Shakespeare.

The man was interested in hiring Bessemer to make a special casting for him. Bessemer was thrilled; he thought he had finally gotten his first major commission. But it was not to be. The sculptor became very sick and died.

Disappointed but determined, Bessemer continued improving his system. Finally he was able to cast using brass on cardboard. Bessemer got his first contract from an art publisher to make 500 casts on cardboard of a painting

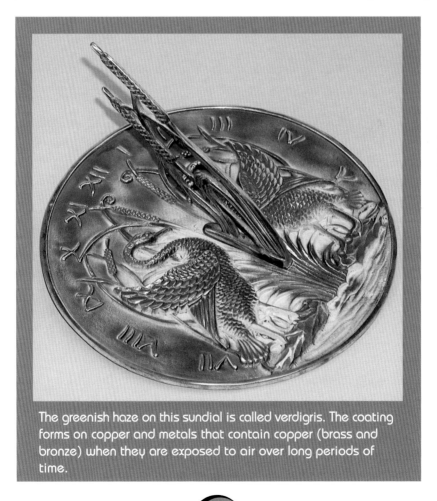

The greenish haze on this sundial is called verdigris. The coating forms on copper and metals that contain copper (brass and bronze) when they are exposed to air over long periods of time.

by renaissance artist Raphael. Even though his die-cast business was enjoying modest success, Bessemer never stopped looking for new projects to challenge his mind.

In the course of his continual experiments, Bessemer wrote, he "discovered another and distinctly different mode of making, from an embossed paper stamp, dies which were capable of reproducing thousands of facsimile impressions. I at once saw to what a dangerous result this discovery might lead if made known to unscrupulous persons."[1] He was specifically imagining counterfeiters.

Thinking he might be able to both serve his country and profit from it, Bessemer painstakingly created casts from which he made counterfeit official government stamps, or seals, used on legal documents. Forgeries were a particular problem in England at the time. Bessemer intended to show the government how to make a stamp that couldn't be mass produced.

Visions of wealth danced in Bessemer's head. "Confident of success, I set to work to make a die for parchment deeds on my new plan, for the time putting aside and neglecting everything else, for this grand project was to make my fortune at once."[2] Bessemer, who had been engaged for two years, hoped to make enough money to finally get married.

He arranged a meeting with the president of the stamp office and showed up full of optimism, expecting to be treated like a hero. Once again, Bessemer was to be bitterly disappointed, this time not because they didn't use his work—they did—but because he was not compensated for his findings. Decades later he would write in his autobiography, "One of the plans I brought before the Stamp Office authorities was adopted by them, and has been to this day employed as a security against forgery on every stamp issued by the Stamp Office during the last half century; but I was nevertheless pushed from pillar to post, and denied all remuneration for the important services I had rendered. I was too busy making my way in life at this period to press any legal claims on the Government. I had no friend at Court, and had to bear this shameful treatment as best I could."[3]

Bessemer's way of dealing with the dissappointment was to go back to inventing. His interests kept expanding, and he found himself moving from one project to another, always in search of the one thing he could settle on as a full-time business. He built a machine that more efficiently cut the graphite used in making pencils, which made pencils much more affordable. He sold the rights to his invention for just $300 to a friend, who in turn would make a profitable arrangement with the company that controlled the graphite mine.

In 1834, Bessemer (who was 21 years old) still did not have enough money to buy a house. He and his fiancée decided to get married anyway. They moved into a residence near Henry's workshop. Finally, in 1840, he would come up with the invention that would make him financially secure.

It started when his sister asked for a simple favor. Henry was a talented calligrapher, and she asked him to paint a title on the portfolio holding her collection of paintings. Henry decided to use gold paint but was taken aback by how expensive gold powder was. The brass that was used to make the powder was cheap, but the process—making it by hand—was not. In 1840 Henry built a machine that would make bronze powder. The machine was a huge success and made Bessemer a rich man. Now he had the freedom to pursue his love of inventing without having to worry about money.

Once he had fortune, Bessemer could concentrate on securing his fame. He entered a competition sponsored by Prince Albert, Queen Victoria's husband, to see who could build a machine that would improve the efficiency of extracting juice from sugarcane, an important crop in England's West Indies colonies. Bessemer's cane press won the competition. When he was presented his gold medal by Prince Albert, he believed it to be the pinnacle of his career.

But Bessemer would soon reach new heights. Just a few years later, he would invent a process that would secure his place as one of the greatest inventors in history.

The 19th century was a golden era for inventions. Engineers, entrepreneurs, and scientists all over the world developed technologies that would lay the foundation for great advances in science, medicine, and manufacturing. But just as important were the inventions that simply made daily life easier. Below are some of the more enduring inventions of the 1800s.

The invention of the tin can sparked the food packaging industry.

1810: Peter Durand of England helped establish the modern food packaging industry when he patented a container for preserving food called "tin cans." Durand's cans were iron layered with a coat of tin, which prevented rust. Within three years, the British military had begun to use Durand's invention because of how long food could be stored in them. The one drawback was that the cans were so thick they could only be opened with a chisel and hammer. As the design improved, the cans became thinner, which led Ezra Warner of Waterbury, Connecticut, to patent the first can opener in 1858. U.S. troops used these can openers during the Civil War.

1827: English chemist John Walker discovered that when he coated small sticks with antimony sulfide, potassium chlorate, gum, and starch and let it dry, he could start a fire by striking the stick against any rough surface. Walker had invented "friction matches." Because he failed to patent the invention, Walker never gained financially from an invention that would eventually be used the world over.

1849: New York mechanic Walter Hunt was trying to figure out a way to repay a $15 debt. He took some wire and bent it into a shape that allowed it to fasten at one end. He called his invention the safety pin and patented it. Thinking there wouldn't be too much use for his invention, he sold the patent for $400. Even though Hunt was a clever inventor, he was a poor businessman. Fifteen years earlier he had built America's first sewing machine, but decided against patenting the design. He feared it would cause too much unemployment if it went into widespread use. This decision allowed Elias Howe to patent the design in 1846 and wrongly take credit for it. Finally, in the 1850s, a court officially named Hunt the inventor.

The Prince and Princess of Wales watch the production of steel at the Cyclops Works in 1875. The steelworks was established in 1845 by Charles Cammell & Co. Ltd. to produce railway springs, wheels, and axles. In the 1860s the company started using the Bessemer process to produce steel rails.

4

The Bessemer Process

With the profits from mechanizing the production of bronze powder, Bessemer moved into a larger factory space. It was there that he built a more efficient glass furnace. The furnace moved the molten glass onto rollers, which would make sheets of glass. This was another successful creation. He sold the invention to a glass manufacturing company for $9,000, which is the equivalent to almost $200,000 in today's money.

In 1854, England and France joined Turkey against Russia in the Crimean War. The conflict started after Czar Nicholas I moved troops into what is now Romania. It got its name because the battles were concentrated on the Crimean Peninsula in the Black Sea.

With his country at war, Bessemer wondered if there was anything he might contribute. It occurred to him that the accuracy of the British military's cannons might be improved by using a rocket-shaped artillery shell instead of a traditional round ball. Bessemer contacted the British War Office and was surprised that nobody there was interested in his invention.

However, the French leader, Napoléon III, was intrigued. Because France was an ally in the war, Bessemer showed Napoléon his new artillery design. But while in France, Bessemer discovered a critical problem. The longer shell weighed more than a comparable round ball. More force would be needed to propel the shell out of the cannon. The cast-iron cannons were not sturdy enough to handle that kind of force—they would break.

It was not the design of the cannon that was the problem; it was the fact that cast iron was very brittle. Cast iron is a type of iron that contains a relatively high amount of carbon, about 4 percent. On the other hand, wrought iron had all the carbon removed. It was very expensive because the process used to remove the carbon was time-consuming. Also, wrought iron was soft and bent easily.

What Bessemer needed was something as easy to work with as wrought iron but strong enough to make the cannon capable of firing his artillery shell. Steel seemed to be the ideal solution. But steel, which is about 1.5 percent carbon, was also very expensive. It required a great deal of costly fuel to keep the metal molten while purifying it. Because it had to be made in a furnace, steel could only be made in 50 pound batches, which wasn't enough to build a cannon.

Charles Bonaparte was the nephew of Napoléon Bonaparte. After being elected president of France, Charles overthrew the government. He named himself emperor and took the title Napoléon III. His desire to protect France's interests in Asia Minor led him to join Britain in the Crimean War against Russia, which was a great victory for France. But after his capture in the 1870–71 war against Prussia, Charles was removed as emperor. He fled to England and died in exile in 1873.

Bessemer started experimenting to see whether he could make cast iron stronger by mixing it with steel. During his experiments, he had an exciting idea. He knew that combining carbon with oxygen gives off heat. He wondered if, when purifying iron, the released carbon combining with the oxygen in the air could produce enough heat to keep the resulting pure iron in liquid form. He devised an experiment to test his theory. To his happy surprise, it worked.

The result was that cast iron could be made into pure iron without having to go through the time-consuming batch process. More importantly, by stopping the process of removing the carbon at the right time, Bessemer would be able to make cast steel. This was a monumental breakthrough that would literally change the world.

As it turned out, Bessemer wasn't the only one to discover that air could be used as a natural fuel in the steelmaking process. In the United States, a Kentucky man named William Kelly had bought an iron forge that was used to convert high-carbon iron into good-quality wrought iron, which he used to manufacture kettles. When local supplies of coal began running low, Kelly started looking for ways to produce higher-quality steel at a lower cost.

One day he realized that air blowing on the molten iron was making it even hotter. He discovered that the carbon in the molten iron would act as a fuel when air blew over it. Unfortunately, Kelly's customers didn't believe that his new process could work. When he wasn't able to find anyone willing to invest in his new system, Kelly was forced to revert to the traditional purifying method using coal. Meanwhile, he continued working on his discovery. Between 1851 and 1856, he built seven different "converters" that had holes in the bottom to blow air into the molten pig, or unpurified, iron.

Kelly was stunned to learn in 1856 that Bessemer had been granted a U.S. patent on the same process and was applying for patents all across Europe as well. He immediately applied for his own patent for what he called the "pneumatic process" and opposed Bessemer's patent with the U.S.

Patent Office. Kelly won, and in June 1857 he was granted the patent and declared the original inventor of the process. The U.S. Patent Office then rescinded Bessemer's patent for the process.

It would be a hollow victory for Kelly. A national financial crisis, which put many banks out of business, led to an economic depression that bankrupted Kelly. Needing money, he sold his patent to his father for $1,000. To Kelly's dismay, his father later refused to sell the patent back to him. Instead his father left the patent to Kelly's sisters. Finally Kelly was able to convince an investor at Cambria Iron Works, which would later be bought by Bethlehem Steel, to help him build another converter. This one was a success and was soon producing inexpensive steel in large quantities for the first time.

Eventually, Kelly's patent would come under the control of Alex L. Holley, which just so happened to be the sole licensee of Bessemer's process. That's how this system for making steel would become known simply as the "Bessemer process," with William Kelly fading into historical obscurity.

Even if Kelly had come up with the idea of using air to rid iron of impurities, Bessemer would take the process several steps further. But first he had to overcome some early obstacles. After his triumphant announcement of his new process, five companies paid Bessemer to use it. According to James Mitchell, former president of the Iron and Steel Institute, the initial results were disastrous. "Brittle when cold, unworkable when hot, the metal produced showed no resemblance to the sample bars which Bessemer had made in his trial furnace and which he had exhibited with such justifiable pride at the British Association Meeting."[1]

Bessemer was in shock. He realized his professional reputation was on the line. Determined to unravel the mystery of why these other companies could not duplicate his results, Bessemer spent the next two years and huge sums of his own money to find the answer and prove to the world that his process could work.

Eventually, Bessemer discovered the reason his process had not worked. The type of pig iron being used in England at the time was high in phosphorus and sulfur. For his process to work properly, those impurities had to be removed.

Even though Bessemer gave his assurance that the mystery was solved, companies were reluctant to try his system again. Setting out to prove them wrong, Bessemer decided to go into the steelmaking business for himself.

Robert Mushet

Besides Henry Bessemer and William Kelly, there were many others who contributed to the development of modern steel production. Robert Mushet was one of those who played a crucial part in the development of Bessemer's process.

Robert Mushet

Because Bessemer's method did not remove phosphorus from the pig iron, only certain kinds of ore could be used. Ores without phosphorus were rare and very expensive, so much of the early steel had limited strength. Since most steel needed to be shaped into some form before it could be used, and phosphorus made the steel brittle, cracks and weaknesses were common.

Like his father before him, Robert Mushet was a metallurgist. While working as an ironmaster in the Forest of Dean in Gloucestershire, England, he conducted a number of experiments to improve the quality of manufactured steel.

In 1856, Mushet found that adding a small amount of an alloy called spiegeleisen—which contained primarily manganese, plus a little carbon—to the molten metal made the Bessemer process work more efficiently. Twelve years later, in 1868, based on this knowledge, Mushet would invent tungsten steel. Tools made from this type of steel lasted up to six times longer than those made without manganese.

However, Mushet would end up never making any money on his invention. Knowing the value of his process, in order to protect his patent, Mushet was very secretive and only a handful of people knew what his mysterious ingredient was. Through a series of unfortunate events, he eventually lost the patents, which allowed Bessemer to incorporate his method without having to pay him. By the 1890s, Bessemer was a millionaire while Mushet was in deep debt. At the urging of Mushet's daughter, Lisowna Mary, Bessemer paid off all of Mushet's debts. However, he never publicly acknowledged Mushet's contribution to his success.

Henry Bessemer became recognized as one of Britain's greatest inventors. He was knighted in 1879. This portrait was made the following year.

5

An Industrial Revolution

Unable to convince anyone to adopt his process, Bessemer set out to build his own steelworks. With the help of some friends, with whom he went into partnership, he was able to buy some land in Sheffield, an industrial region that was home to many other ironworks and steel manufacturers. He called the new company Henry Bessemer & Company, and it started production in 1859 using Swedish pig iron. His goal wasn't so much to start a new business as it was to simply show people that his process worked.

Initially the company was only able to produce small quantities of steel, but it gradually increased its output. Because of how much money he was able to save on fuel, Bessemer was soon able to sell his steel for $30 less per ton than any of his competitors. Realizing that they could not compete with Bessemer and would go out of business if they continued making steel the old way, companies quickly began taking out licenses to use the Bessemer process. In 1860, John Brown was the first to license the process. In all, Bessemer would be paid over $1 million in licensing fees, which would be almost $19 million today.

The investment would have been worth it. Bessemer's process was said to be 10 times faster than the batch process and could make 30 tons at once, compared to 50 pounds per batch. Ever the inventor, Bessemer designed machinery to improve the efficiency of steelmaking, including a tilting converter. Using his process and designs, steel companies were suddenly able to produce large quantities of inexpensive steel that could be used for construction, railways, armor, and precision tools. In 1850, annual British steel production was approximately 50,000 tons. By 1880, production of Bessemer steel would reach 1,000,000 tons.

Bessemer's discovery could not have come at a more opportune time. After the end of the Crimean War in 1856, the demand for steel had started to grow as more railroads were being built and the military looked to produce more and better armaments.

As important as the Bessemer method was in Britain, it would take on even greater significance elsewhere in the world, especially in the United States. Andrew Carnegie, who founded U.S. Steel, traveled frequently to England and was impressed with the converter Bessemer had built. Carnegie correctly predicted that steel would become the material of choice for heavy construction. In 1874, Carnegie opened his

Andrew Carnegie was a Scottish immigrant who became the world's richest man. The son of a weaver, Andrew's family moved to America when he was 13. Carnegie made his fortune in steel, founding the Carnegie Steel Company, which he eventually sold for $480 million. A lifelong philanthropist, Carnegie spent the rest of his life working for various causes and would spend over $56 million building public libraries.

first steel furnace that incorporated Bessemer's process. He was able to supply steel for America's rapidly expanding railway system. By the early 20th century, steel would be used to build everything from ships to skyscrapers to bridges. And as American steel production increased, the Bessemer process underwent improvements and modifications to make it even more efficient.

Now that his reputation and place in history were assured, Bessemer set out to correct a wrong he felt had been dealt him all those years ago by the stamp office. In

November 1878, he wrote a lengthy, angry letter to the Prime Minister. He outlined the outrage he had felt because he had never been fairly compensated for supplying the office with the system to prevent counterfeiting.

The Prime Minister wrote back, agreeing a disservice had been done and that Bessemer should be compensated. In addition, the Prime Minister would push for Bessemer to receive one of Britain's greatest honors. In his autobiography, Bessemer relates, "On the 21st June I received an intimation . . . that Her Most Gracious Majesty had been pleased to signify her intention of conferring on me the honor of Knighthood."[1]

The ceremony was held at Windsor Castle. A royal carriage was sent to pick up Bessemer. Using a jewel-encrusted sword, Queen Victoria knighted Bessemer, who in turn was required to kiss her hand. After the ceremony and lunch at the castle, the inventor returned to London as *Sir* Henry Bessemer.

Bessemer, who never lost his natural inquisitiveness, continued to invent throughout his life. One of his last inventions was prompted by the fact that he suffered from sea sickness. He designed a system that kept a ship cabin steady. In his later years Bessemer spent his days looking through his telescope, developing a method to cut and polish lenses, refurbishing his home, and building a diamond-cutting plant. He died on March 14, 1898.

Bessemer was one of the last general inventors. During his lifetime he held 117 patents. Although he always had great vision and belief in himself, it's doubtful that even he could have known just how important his steelmaking process would be to civilization. In *The Life of Andrew Carnegie*, Burton J. Hendrick quoted engineer Abraham S. Hewitt as saying, "The Bessemer invention takes rank with the great events which have changed the face of society since the Middle Ages. The invention of printing, the construction of the magnetic compass, the discovery of America and the introduction of the steam engine are the only capital events in modern history which belong to the same category as the Bessemer Process."[2]

Hendrick credited Bessemer for, "preparing the way for the higher civilization."[3] Bessemer's process was the foundation for the Industrial Revolution, which transformed modern civilization and paved the way for the great technological advances we enjoy today.

Central Pacific and Union Pacific railway lines nearly touching

Thanks to Bessemer's work, navies around the world were radically transformed. For centuries, sailing ships had been made primarily of wood. The designs of ships underwent dramatic changes with the introduction of iron and steel hulls. Once it was possible to mass-produce steel, shipbuilders could construct much larger vessels capable of carrying massive amounts of cargo compared to their smaller wooden cousins. And whereas sailing ships relied on the wind for power, the new steel-hulled ships were powered by steam engines that had propellers attached.

Nowhere was the efficiency of this new class of ship more valued than in the military, where wooden sailboats had long been used to transport armies and carry small firearms during conflicts. Steel-hulled battleships could be heavily armed with multiple gun turrets and cannons.

Another important event in the United States during the 19th century was the completion of the Transcontinental Railroad. Although the dream of a shore-to-shore railway had first been discussed in the 1830s, it wasn't until two decades later, when the California gold rush attracted massive numbers of settlers to the West, that such an undertaking was seriously considered. Without Bessemer's process, sturdy, long-lasting rails wouldn't have been possible.

In 1862, Congress passed the Pacific Railroad Bill, which gave money and land so that the Union Pacific Railroad could build west from Missouri, and the Central Pacific Line could build east from California. For the next six years, the two companies would overcome unfavorable weather, labor disputes, Native American resistance, disease, political corruption, and financial problems to keep the project going.

On May 10, 1869, with the locomotives from the Central Pacific and Union Pacific lines nearly touching, the final spikes, made of gold, were driven into the rails as people on both coasts "listened" to the event via telegraph operators who reported the event live. For the first time in American history, the United States was truly joined from sea to shining sea.

Chronology

1813	Born January 19 in Charlton, Hertfordshire, England
1830	Moves to London; establishes personal business to sell art works; develops anti-forgery embossed stamps
1834	Marries the daughter of his best friend
1840	Discovers how to create gold paint by using bronze
1841	Takes out patent for new method of manufacturing glass
1850	Wins the Royal Society of Arts Albert Medal for inventing the cane press
1854	Invents new type of artillery shell, but the military is unable to use it
1855	Patents the Bessemer process
1859	Establishes steel mill in Sheffield, England
1877	Is elected to the Royal Society of London
1879	Is knighted by Queen Victoria
1898	Dies March 15 in London
1905	Bessemer's autobiography is published by the Offices of Engineering in London

Timeline of Discovery

1803	The United States buys Louisiana Territory from France.
1807	Robert Fulton introduces the first steamboat.
1814	Francis Scott Key writes "The Star-Spangled Banner."
1837	Samuel Morse invents the telegraph.
1851	Isaac Merritt Singer begins manufacturing Singer sewing machines.
1854–56	The Crimean War is fought.
1857	William Kelly patents his converter for making steel.
1859	Charles Darwin publishes *The Origin of the Species.*
1861	American Civil War starts.
1864	Jules Verne's *Journey to the Center of the Earth* is published.
1866	Alfred Nobel produces dynamite.
1876	Alexander Graham Bell invents the telephone.
1879	Thomas Alva Edison invents the incandescent lamp.
1884	Hiram Maxim invents the machine gun.
1885	In Chicago, William Le Baron Jenney builds the first skyscraper.
1889	Gustav Eiffel completes the Eiffel Tower; George A. Fuller's Tacoma Building is completed in Chicago.
1899	Felix Hoffman produces aspirin.
1903	The Wright brothers make the first powered flight.
1908	Henry Ford mass-produces the Model T.

Chapter Notes

Chapter One   **Reaching for the Sky**

    1. Ivar Lissner, *The Living Past,* translated by J. Maxwell Brownjohn (New York: Putnam's, 1957), p. 82.

Chapter Two   **Inquisitive by Nature**

    1. Sir Henry Bessemer, *An Autobiography,* http://www.bibliomania.com/2/9/71/118/21360/1/frameset.htm, Chapter 1, pps. 3–4.

    2. Ibid., p. 4.

    3. Ibid.

    4. Ibid., p. 5.

Chapter Three   **A Prolific Inventor**

    1. Sir Henry Bessemer, *An Autobiography,* http://www.bibliomania.com/2/9/71/118/21360/1/frameset.htm, Chapter 2, p. 1.

    2. Ibid., p. 2.

    3. Ibid., p. 4.

Chapter Four   **The Bessemer Process**

    1. James Mitchell, "The Bessemer Centenary Lecture," http://www.corusrail125.co.uk/Sir%20Henry%20Bessemer.htm

Chapter Five   **An Industrial Revolution**

    1. Sir Henry Bessemer, *An Autobiography,* http://www.bibliomania.com/2/9/71/118/21360/1/frameset.htm, Chapter 2, p. 10.

    2. Burton J. Hendrick, *The Life of Andrew Carnegie* (London: Heinemann, 1933), p. 134.

    3. Ibid.

Further Reading

For Young Adults

Barraclough, Kenneth C. *Steel-making Before Bessemer.* London: Metals Society, 1984.

Collins, Mary. *The Industrial Revolution.* Cornerstones of Freedom. Danbury, Connecticut: Children's Press, 2000.

Rau, Dana Meachen. *Andrew Carnegie: Captain of Industry.* Signature Lives. Minneapolis: Compass Point Books, 2005.

Whiting, Jim. *James Watt and the Steam Engine.* Hockessin, Delaware: Mitchell Lane Publishers, 2006.

Works Consulted

Bessemer, Sir Henry. *An Autobiography.* London: Maney Publishing, 1989. Also available on the internet: http://www.bibliomania.com/2/9/71/118/21360/1/frameset.html

Bodsworth, C. *Sir Henry Bessemer: Father of the Steel Industry.* London: Maney Publishing, 1989.

Carr, J.C. *History of the British Steel Industry.* Cambridge: Harvard University Press, 1962.

Fisher, Douglas Alan. *Steel: From the Iron Age to the Space Age.* New York: Harper Collins, 1967.

Hendrick, Burton J. *The Life of Andrew Carnegie.* London: Heinemann, 1933.

Lissner, Ivar. *The Living Past,* translated by J. Maxwell Brownjohn. New York: Putnam's, 1957.

On the Internet

Greater London Industrial Archeological Society, http://www.glias.org.uk/news/212news.html

Hart-Davis, Adam. "Henry Bessemer, Man of Steel," http://www.exnet.com/1995/09/27/science/science.html

History for Kids: *Steel,* http://www.historyforkids.org/learn/science/steel.htm

Lucidcafe: *Henry Bessemer English Inventor and Engineer,* http://www.lucidcafe.com/lucidcafe/library/96jan/bessemer.html

Mitchell, James. "The Bessemer Centenary Lecture," http://www.corusrail125.co.uk/Sir%20Henry%20Bessemer.htm

Glossary

brass   a metal made of copper mixed with zinc.

bronze   a metal made of copper mixed with tin.

calligrapher   (cah-LIH-gruh-fer)—someone who can write with artistic, elegant, or stylized penmanship.

font   (fahnt)—a collection of typefaces that share similar design features.

forge   (forj)—a furnace used to heat metal so that it can be formed.

lathe   (laythe)—a tool used to spin metal or wood so that a worker can shape it.

metallurgy   (MEH-tul-ur-jee)—the science of metals, including their properties and uses.

pig iron   (PIG eye-rn)—unrefined iron.

pipeclay   (PIPE-clay)—a fine-grained white clay used for making pipes and for whitening leather.

plaster of paris   (PLAS-ter of PAIR-us)—a white powder made of calcium that when mixed with water can be molded or cast and left to harden; it is often used to make sculptures.

type foundry   (TIPE fown-dree)—a company that designs typefaces and produces the metal dies used for printing them.

verdigris   (VAIR-duh-gree)—a greenish blue pigment obtained from copper.

Index